MW00639713

The Seeds of Hope

one woman's physical, emotional, and spiritual victory over cancer

HOPE ALANIZ

Weller & Bunsby
PUBLISHERS

Published by Weller & Bunsby
wellerandbunsby.com

Italics within all Scripture quotations are the author's.

Cover art:
Christie McMillon, True Beauty Photography
Beth Pryor, Pryor Design

I lovingly dedicate this little book to my father and inspiration, Raymond Martinez, who went to meet the Lord on August 26, 2007.

My father had lost a leg to diabetes and walked with the aid of a prosthesis. Three times a week, he went in for dialysis. But he never murmured or complained. The average lifespan of a diabetic patient, once he begins dialysis, is three years. My father continued to receive treatments for fourteen years!

His pastor cried during the funeral service. Ray, he said, would come to church in ice, snow, sleet, or rain. He explained how my father embedded a nail in the tip of his crutch to keep himself from slipping on the ice. But I doubt that it was the nail that kept him on his feet. I suspect that his angels kept close watch over him when he was going back and forth to church and the hospital or running errands.

And as long as he lived, he prayed for my healing.

So I thank both of my fathers—my dad and my God, now in heaven together—for taking such good care of me.

foreword

ONE NIGHT in a dream, the Holy Spirit told me to start writing about the journey I took with God after I was diagnosed with cancer.

In the dream, I saw myself writing furiously. Thoughts and words flowed out of me into my computer. I experienced an urgent desire to express my prayers, dreams, thoughts, and hopes in the book. And as I did, I felt elated.

But my conscious mind struggled against the dream.

"No," I thought, "I can't start writing a book. I'm still working. I don't have time."

Then, in my spirit, I heard the voice again.

"Start writing your testimony now," he said, "because you are going to retire very soon."

Within a couple of weeks, my retirement was approved. God had opened a door for me to share my message of hope and his faithfulness.

I pray that this little book helps you in your battle against cancer or any other disease or infirmity.

Your walk with God through the shadows may not be the same as mine. In fact, it probably won't be, because he has something special for you, just as he did for me.

Just be encouraged by my journey. Then, be still and listen for his voice.

1
diagnosis

CANCER! What an ugly word!

I watched two sisters-in-law fight cancer, and I sometimes wondered how I would react if it ever happened to me. I saw them go through denial and fear.

I saw the physical and spiritual strength drain out of them. And not only them, but the rest of the family, as well.

We all had put so much energy into caring for our loved ones, knowing that the outcome would not be good. Again and again, we wrestled alongside them with sadness, hopelessness, and anger.

Then, at the end of 2003, I experienced some symptoms that worried me.

I had been having bladder problems and frequent urinary tract infections. I was beginning to feel pain and see bright drops of blood every time I went to the bathroom.

I knew I needed to see a doctor.

My family physician referred me to a specialist, but he wasn't accepting new patients. So he recommended another, who also wasn't taking on new patients, and then another.

I prayed that the Lord would guide me to the right doctor, and he was so faithful.

He finally put a Christian urologist/surgeon in my path and threw open the door.

The first step was to have a biopsy, to cut out a piece of the tumor, send it to the lab, and have it checked for cancer.

I was very nervous when the anesthesiologist came to put me to sleep. In my heart, I knew that something was seriously wrong, and I had started weeping. He tried to comfort me, told me that the procedure would be over soon, and placed the mask over my nose and mouth. I felt as though a warm blanket was being draped over me, and I let myself go with it.

At the same time, my sister-in-law Mary was praying over the phone with my son, Mike and nephew, Jose, asking God to provide me with a *blanket* of protection. Our Father is so faithful!

After the surgery, when I returned home, I noticed a huge lump on the back of my neck. Mike felt it, thought it might be a swollen lymph node, and urged me to tell the doctor.

Before calling, I asked Mike and his wife, Alyssa, to lay their hands on it and pray for it to go away. I also called my sister, Ginger, and asked her to pray.

"Lord," I said, "make it smooth and supple." And I prayed that throughout the night.

In the morning, I reached back to feel my neck. The lump was gone.

I called to Mike and Alyssa in the next room. They could find no trace of it. The lump was completely gone.

I called Ginger to thank her for her fervent prayers.

"How did you make that lump disappear, Lord?" I asked.

And immediately the thought came into my mind that, if God can heal something I can see and feel, he can surely heal something hidden inside my body. That was when I knew that God was my healer. And the lump has never returned.

the dreaded news

The diagnosis was bladder cancer.

The doctor told me to bring my family and a close friend to his office, so we could discuss my treatment options because I would need a lot of support.

I held my husband's hand tightly, trying to squeeze out the energy I needed to help me get through the visit, trying to draw from Marc strength that I knew I didn't have.

My first reaction was fear. Then I thought about dying. And that was the start of an emotional roller coaster that would crawl up and swoop down and rattle and roar and screech throughout my entire experience.

Spiritually and emotionally, I was totally caught off guard. But God wasn't.

Before we left the office that day, the doctor, my family members, my dear friend Patsy and I held hands and prayed for my healing.

That was a special time. And after the doctor finished praying for me, I prayed for him and his practice and asked the Lord to bless him.

The most baffling part of the illness was that I didn't fall into any of the categories of people who are likely to get the disease.

I didn't smoke, drink, or work with carcinogenic chemicals. And I was aware of no history of cancer in my family.

How could this happen to me? I always stayed on top of my health issues and had regular checkups.

My doctor told me that only one other patient in his office had the same kind of cancer and that she didn't fall into any of those categories either.

I asked him for her first name so that I could pray for her healing, too.

He said it was Linda. Praying for Linda helped her, I am sure, and it also helped me to keep my focus off of myself.

Marc and I had driven to the doctor's office in separate cars because he had just had surgery, was in pain, and needed to get home as soon as he could. So Patsy said she would ride home with me.

On the way, we stopped at our church to ask one of the pastors to pray with us for healing. And Patsy and I continued to pray the rest of the way home.

We told Satan he did not have the right to invade my body, soul, or health. We prayed fervently to the Lord and asked him to heal me, standing on his promises and asking him for comfort and peace during this trial.

After we finished praying, I told Patsy that I felt something had changed. I felt separate from myself.

It was almost as if I was looking down at myself. Patsy assured me that it was the effect of the Holy Spirit, who had come to comfort me in my time of need.

The rest of the day, I did a lot of thinking. Did God allow Satan to afflict me? Was this a test of my faith? I didn't know what God's plans were for me, but I did know that he loved me and would be with me every step of the way.

I decided then and there that I was going to totally trust him. No questioning. No defiance. No looking back. I set myself to move forward and put up a ferocious fight.

No matter what happened, whether I lived or died, I was determined to win. I would beat the disease with all of God's help or die trusting him and step into eternal life with him. Either way, alive or dead, I would win.

refusal, not denial

The first thing I did was to detach myself from the disease. It was not *my* cancer. I wasn't in denial, but I didn't accept it either. I just kept reminding myself that God is bigger than cancer, which I was certain he would crumple up like a wad of paper and throw into the lake of fire. I continued to renew my mind by focusing on my healthy cells, the ones that would do the frontline battle against the cancer cells.

Before falling asleep at night, I imagined God breathing healing particles of light into my nostrils. The Holy Spirit helped by blocking negative thoughts about the disease. I kept thinking to myself:

> *I am well. I am healthy. I can feel God's healing light inside my body. I will sleep well, not worry, and empty my soul, spirit, and body of any harmful thoughts. I will rid myself of all emotional garbage.*

Just because I was sick didn't mean that God didn't want me to continue working with him to advance his kingdom. So I continued to pray for others at every opportunity.

I began my walk of faith, believing that my prayers had already been answered, just as Jesus promised when he said, "whatever you ask for in prayer, believe that you have received it, and it will be yours."[1]

The next morning, I arrived at work and prepared to face the day and tell my supervisor about my diagnosis. I did not feel dread or sadness. On the contrary, I felt elated and joyful.

Wait a minute. Did I say elated and joyful? Yes! That's exactly how I felt. I was walking on clouds.

I went into my supervisor's office and explained to him that I had been diagnosed with cancer. He looked at me kind of funny, no doubt because I was smiling and happy.

And, no, I wasn't on medication. I was just joyful. Do you know why? Because I knew that God was going to heal me. I felt it in my spirit, in my soul, and in my whole being.

I was not frightened anymore. I was going to do exactly what the devil did not want me to do. I was going to open up my house, let the light in, receive visitors, be prayed over, and read Scripture.

I knew that the promises in the Bible were true and that God would shrink the disease and increase my healthy cells.

I also told a co-worker about my diagnosis. I shared my thoughts with her and told her how I was feeling. She was going through some issues at work and shared them with me. So I prayed for her.

---

[1] Mark 11:24 NIV.

"Hope," she said afterward, "*you're* the one who's sick. I should be praying for *you*."

But I knew that God wanted me to give back. To share the love and comfort he was pouring into me, to take my attention off myself and share the faith that was sustaining me.

Today, that co-worker has a special place in my heart because I know that God touched her that day and that I was the vessel he used to do it.

I also knew that I had a long road ahead. But I was going to put on my breastplate of righteousness and my helmet of salvation.[2] I would live one day at a time and expect healing. This sickness would be temporary. And I didn't have to fight alone.

---

[2] Ephesians 6:13-18.

2
chemotherapy

I KNEW THAT chemical therapy destroys good cells as well as bad. And I had heard plenty of horror stories from my sisters-in-law as they went through the treatment. But I was determined to displace those thoughts with the truth of God's word.

I began by thanking God for giving scientists the knowledge to develop medicine that would help kill cancer cells.

Then, every time those powerful chemicals were pumped into my body, I thought of Jesus on the cross, which made my ordeal appear less painful and less tragic.

My mind felt as though it would burst as I tried to imagine how God felt when he knew that his Son would have to become a man, be tortured, shamed, and executed as a base criminal, and die so that I could be reconciled to him.

I also remembered that Jesus said that one of the signs that will follow those who believe is that, if they drink any deadly thing, it will not hurt them.[3]

[3] Mark 16:18.

At least three times a week for four months, I went to the cancer center for chemotherapy treatments. And each time, I looked for opportunities to share some of my comfort and hope with others. Cancer is no respecter of persons. It attacks rich and poor, young and old, uneducated and professional. Every face I saw reflected sadness, fear, or pain.

Once, I struck up a conversation with a lady who sat beside her husband weeping. I introduced myself and asked if it was her first treatment. She said it was her second and that she had been diagnosed with breast cancer. I told her I was on my third treatment and that I was feeling good and happy.

When she asked why, I explained that I had taken time to be still and listen to God's voice. I said that God had told me I was healed and that I could feel it in my spirit and soul. She said she believed in God and went to church, but that God had not spoken to her. Encouraged by my testimony, she told me she was going to go home, be still, and listen for his voice.

Whenever I went in for a treatment, I focused on one person and spent the time praying for him or her as a way of thanking God for healing me.

Altogether, I received twenty-four chemotherapy treatments.

I lost all my hair and experienced night sweats, chills, constipation, and fevers. But I was never in pain. And I never complained to my oncologist, who said he wished all his patients had my attitude. I tried to explain that it was the result of my assurance that God had healed me, but he didn't seem to believe me—which was okay, because I knew that God would have the last word.

This is not to say that I didn't experience sadness and depression. They're a normal side effect of the chemicals. But I never had to ask for medication to help me cope with those feelings. I just prayed my way through them, like King David did when he was sad or depressed.[4]

"Why are you looking down?" I asked my soul. "Lift your head up, and see the light in the darkness!"

I continued to work full-time throughout my course of treatments. Every morning, I got up, put a smile on my face, and dove into the day's challenges. And instead of worrying, I prayed.

"It's only temporary," I reminded myself. "Take the treatments one at a time, and enjoy every day that you don't have to have a treatment."

My pastor always told us that we can be our own best counselors when we're going through hard times. And he was right.

---

[4] Psalm 142:5-6.

I was reading a book at the time that said, when you're going through something difficult, celebrate. Have a party. So I asked my husband to invite some family and friends over for a barbecue to celebrate my healing. And when the day came, I put on my wig and makeup and dressed to receive our guests.

It was as if God had arranged everything else to make the celebration perfect. The Texas heat broke, and a cool breeze made everything delightful. Everyone we invited came, and they were all amazed at how well I looked. I said of course, because the Lord had healed me, and I was putting my faith into action.

shared struggle

My husband faithfully supported me while I was undergoing treatments. Newly retired, Marc always drove me to the hospital. Then, he sat for hours, worked on his crossword puzzles, brought my lunches, and shared my thoughts with me during the infusion.

I knew it was hard on him. He had to face so many obstacles himself, both physically and spiritually. A disease like cancer has a way of draining those closest to us nearly as much as it drains us. But through all our ups and downs, we walked through it together and came out the other side with a stronger marriage.

3

vision and dreams

THROUGHOUT my journey with the Lord, I was soaked in prayer by co-workers, church members, relatives, friends, and family. I was added to church prayer chains. Even people who didn't know me prayed for me.

Whenever someone called to encourage me, ask how I was feeling, or inquire if there was anything they could do, I urged them to pray for my healing and for others who were going through the same trial.

Just before my first treatment, I had a vision.

I woke up early one morning. The house was quiet. I went into the living room and started praying. I decided to lie on the floor with my arms outstretched and concentrate on listening to the Holy Spirit.

As I lay there, neither asleep nor awake, I seemed to be looking down at me as though I was hovering above myself. And I was surrounded by a circle of people holding hands.

I couldn't see their faces, but I saw that an angel hovered above each person, and the angels, too, were holding hands.

Above the angels and the people was a bright white light that made everything feel warm and safe. Then I heard a voice.

"Hope, you are loved."

That's all it said.

The clock began to chime, and the vision ended, leaving me with assurance that God was listening to all the prayers.

confirmations and encouragements

That was the only vision I had, but I had lots of dreams. The first came after I told my parents about the diagnosis and asked for their prayers.

My father was diabetic and had dialysis treatments on Fridays that left him very weak. So he was unable to handle the four-hour drive to come to see me until the next day. And though my mother, Nettie, was ill and couldn't come with him, I enjoyed my visit with my dad.

That night, I dreamed that I was walking along the driveway that leads to my home. Our house sits in back of the property at the end of a long, winding drive.

On the driveway, I saw a snake. While snakes are pretty common here in Texas, I'd never seen one like this. It was man-sized and man-like, its tongue flicking in and out. It was big, green, and ugly.

Although the snake was poised to strike, I walked toward it. And as I got closer, I realized that I was not afraid.

I walked past the snake and looked directly into its eyes.

It didn't strike at me, and a few feet further on, I turned to see the snake slithering away.

When I woke up Sunday morning, I told my dad about the dream and asked if he could interpret it. He said the snake was the cancer and, because my faith was so strong, I had stared into it and walked past it without fear.

In another dream, I was sitting on the front porch, talking with Jose, Mike, and Alyssa. Suddenly, something caught our attention and we looked into the sky to see what looked like a tornado coming toward us.

We could see through it, and in the middle was a large tree with exposed roots, like the wind had just sucked it out of the ground. It appeared as if we would soon be crushed by the tree, but we weren't afraid.

In an instant, the funnel cloud dropped the tree in front of the house, and it landed perfectly upright and balanced, though the roots were still above ground. So we all got up to look at it.

"Look," I told my nephew, "it's full of fruit."

Then fruit started dropping off the tree, and we picked some off of the low-hanging branches. I was still staring at the tree and tasting the fruit when I awakened.

I felt that the Holy Spirit was telling me that I was in the midst of a storm and, though I felt uprooted and vulnerable, I would come through it healthy and intact.

And my ordeal would produce spiritual fruit.[5]

good dreams and not so good dreams

Throughout the four months of my treatments, I asked God to enable me to sleep and not worry about anything. I knew it was very important for me to get enough rest so I didn't further damage my immune system.

And God is so good. I always slept peacefully. And he continued to comfort, reassure, and encourage me through dreams.

One dream, however, scared me a little.

Again, hovering above the scene, I saw a woman in the woods, tied to a tree. Nearby was a man who wanted to kill her. I couldn't see his face, but I knew he was out of control. He wanted to strangle her. I prayed fervently in tears, pleading with God to protect her.

Then I saw the man walk over to the woman, his hands reaching for her throat. Suddenly, he tripped and fell into a ravine, fracturing his ankle and unable to get up. He was obviously in extreme pain.

Then the woman wriggled free and escaped, leaving her injured assailant behind.

Again, I tried to figure out what God was trying to tell me.

---

[5] Matthew 7:17,20.

In the morning, I even checked the paper to see if anything strange had happened overnight in the city.

Finally, I called my sister-in-law Mary and shared the dream with her, and God gave her the interpretation. She told me that I was the woman tied to the tree (I live in the country), and the would-be murderer was Satan. Fervent prayer was enabling me to escape, and God was giving me my life back.

I also had a recurring dream about writing this little book. But once my treatments were over, the dreams stopped.

I adore and cherish the way God communicated with me. The vision and dreams strengthened me when I was weakest. They nurtured me—heart, mind and soul—and kept hope alive.

4
prayer

DURING THE THIRD month of treatment, my father came again to visit. This time, my mother—a diabetic, like my father, but who also suffered cirrhosis of the liver—and my sister Nita came with him.

My mother was exhausted when they arrived that afternoon and went right to bed. First, however, I felt that God wanted me to pray for her. So we prayed together for our healings.

The next morning, she told me that she had slept very well. What she didn't share the night before was that she was in excruciating pain and had received immediate relief when we prayed, which enabled her to sleep.

As I said before, Marc was very supportive of me throughout the entire cancer ordeal, always by my side. But he was also angry at God. He had lost three sisters to cancer and now felt that the disease had come to claim his wife.

I shared this with a very close friend at church who prayed with me over the phone and told me that my husband needed to ask God for forgiveness.

"Why do I have to ask God for forgiveness?" Marc asked.

I said that I didn't think God would heal me unless he was free from anger. He thought about this, and we didn't talk about it anymore.

I know he listened to me and dealt with God on his own terms. And the morning before my major surgery, when Marc prayed for me, I could see that he'd had his talk with God.

prayed-for people pray for people

Prayer is amazingly powerful, I believe, when a sick person looks outside himself or herself to pray for another sick person.

I was especially blessed by the prayers of a woman who was introduced to me by a mutual friend. She too was battling cancer and wanted to pray with me for my healing. We spent hours praying together over the phone and discussing God's power to heal. And I know that our prayers helped one another.

A co-worker also asked me to speak to her sister who lived out of state and had just been diagnosed with lymphoma.

Through phone calls and emails, I encouraged her to believe that she was going to get well and not to profess anything else.

I helped her to think more positively about her illness and asked God to give her the strength to move forward.

She told me that she had been so uplifted that she wished I lived close by.

God used my illness to put me in contact with so many people.

My niece Christie's grandmother, Helen, had just been healed from cancer. I had never met her, but she wrote, shared many powerful Scripture verses, and prayed that God would heal me, too. And her strength strengthened me.

While I was sick, I used my down time to pray alone, frequently outdoors where I felt especially close to God.

One day, Mike suggested that we plant a garden to help me focus my thoughts on life and growth while I was healing.

So we did, and that vegetable garden produced the most luscious, delicious tomatoes, vibrant green peppers, and beautiful eggplants I had ever tasted.

I delighted in watching them grow at the same time that I was healing, and we all enjoyed its fruits.

In addition to prayer, I focused on God's promises for healing.

Again and again, I read the Psalms, etching their beautiful words in my mind.

Oh, before I forget, do you remember the other patient my doctor said had the same kind of cancer?

I had continued to pray for her, and one day, I met a woman at the center and, as we talked, I discovered that it was Linda.

We talked, and I was able to share my faith in fighting the disease and let her know that I had been praying for her.

I can't thank God enough for all the support he provided through friends and family members, even strangers, while I was sick. And I know that not everyone has this kind of support.

But it really all comes down to you and the Lord. And he is more than sufficient.

5
surgery

THE CHEMOTHERAPY treatments, my doctor explained, would not be enough.

He would also have to perform a hysterectomy, remove my bladder, and make a new one out of my intestine. He said I would be in the hospital for about two weeks and then need time to recover.

Major surgery! What are you talking about? Remove my bladder? Hysterectomy? I am totally not ready for this!

The most major hospital visit I'd ever had was when my children were born.

I went home and prayed.

Lord, how am I going to get through this part of the illness? I don't want to go to sleep for hours and wake up to find body parts missing.

And Satan used my anxiety to full advantage.

I had terrible nightmares, in which I saw myself waking up from surgery, angry, missing body parts, and blaming God for everything.

Then I was mad at my subconscious for allowing me to dream such things that I knew were not from the Lord.

I counseled with my family, friends, coworkers, and spiritual advisors. I knew deep down inside that I would have to go through with the surgery, so I asked God to help me overcome all my negative thoughts and feelings.

love letter

One night, I awoke from a deep sleep. I felt that the Holy Spirit was telling me to get up and write a letter to all the people who had been standing with me all these months.

"Oh no," I said, sleepily, "not now. I'm resting so comfortably, and I want to go back to sleep."

"Get up now," he insisted. "Go sit at the computer and start writing a letter. Let everyone know how God is healing you and how much strength and knowledge God has given you to cope with a disease like this."

I got up and wrote the following letter:

October 16, 2004

Dear Friends, Family, Coworkers, Church:

I am writing this letter to express my deep love and appreciation for all the prayers and support I have received from you during my time of illness. I also want to let you know how I am progressing, the tools I am using to get through this, and how important spirituality has played a role in this recovery process.

As you all know, earlier this year I was diagnosed with bladder cancer. I didn't fit any of the categories for having the disease; the doctor says DNA went crazy in that part of my body. I am the type of person that has always followed up on my medical exams and received yearly exams without failure. My doctor explained that tests confirmed the tumor removed from the biopsy was cancerous and that the disease had invaded the bladder wall. I would have to undergo five months of chemotherapy and have surgery to remove the bladder. I couldn't understand how I got the disease. I was devastated; my life was on the line. I had read all the articles on bladder cancer and how dangerous it was.

The day I received the diagnosis, I was fortunate enough to be in the company of my family and friends. I prayed so hard that day with my close friend. We were in agreement that no disease could be greater than God. And that Satan was a liar and a thief and that he had no place in my life. We just went down the list of Scriptures, If God is for me, who can be against me; Greater is He who is in me than he who in the World; God has not given me a spirit of fear but a spirit of power, love, and a sound mind. At the end of our intense prayer session, I told my friend that I didn't feel like myself anymore. I felt like I was detached from myself. My friend assured me that the Holy Spirit had come to comfort me and be with me during this journey.

I was more emotionally hurt than anything else. I really needed a big band aid for my feelings. What an emotional blow. I thought to myself, now God, I love you. Why is this happening to me? Since becoming a Christian, I never failed to witness your love or pray for others when they were going through trials and tribulations. I always told them how good God was and how powerful prayer was. I wracked my brain trying to figure it all out. Then I had to stop questioning God and tell myself to stop trying to reason it. I figured out that only God knew and that I may never know why the disease attacked me. God is God and I'm not. God may have allowed Satan to attack me as a test for my faith (as he did to Job) or it may have been an attack from Satan. I just don't know and may never know. I had to move on to the next step.

I thought to myself, now how am I going to fight this disease? The first thing that came to my mind was "be anxious for nothing". Do not worry about anything. Do not use any negative energy. Clean your body spiritually, if you want God to heal you. Do not harbor any anger, resentment, jealousy, or animosity towards anyone. Do not be ashamed. Be open about this illness and ask your friends and family to pray for you and use this positive energy to bathe yourself in divine prayer. The prayers will go up to heaven where God will receive them and they will come back down on earth where you will absorb them. Take all that love, prayer, support, continue to do God's work, and send it back to others.

I'm at the point where I have completed the chemotherapy. During chemotherapy, I asked God to specifically allow me to eat and sleep well. And I slept well. I would go to bed at night imagining God repairing my cells, God breathing particles of light and divine power and energy in my body. I have experienced supernatural dreams and visions, which I will share with you later. I experienced no fear, doubts, or worry. I slept soundly and peacefully. I did have discomforts and many a time I'd be hanging my head over the toilet, feeling just awful, praising God, and thanking Jesus for taking the harshest pain because He loved us so much. God wants us to praise Him during the good times and bad times (one of the many things I've learned from my Pastor). I just have to pass this test. I will not let Him down. I refuse to blame God or be angry at Him.

The oncology doctor is amazed how well I went through the chemotherapy and was still able to work. I witnessed to him every chance I had. He looked at me like I was in left field because modern day medicine only teaches science and spirituality virtually has no role in recovery of disease. But that's OK. I just had to let him know that I was not going through this by myself. That there was a much greater power guiding me.

I've just completed a round of tests. The CAT scan I took a couple of weeks ago shows no tumor. All of the other tests have come back clean. The doctor says, as a major precautionary measure, I still have to have surgery for removal of the bladder because 70% of the time there are still microscopic cells in the bladder wall. Something no biopsy can reveal. I feel confident that God knows every hair on my head, every cell in my body, all about my physical makeup, and has taken care of that situation. I am healed. If God has answered my prayers for others He can do it for me also. I have a decision to make about having the surgery and I want my decision to be crystal clear. I need your help in praying that I will make the right decision.

I also want to thank you for all your powerful prayers, concerns, phone calls, cards, and love during this time. It has made me so much stronger and I feel all your divine energy. I feel like I'm wearing a coat of prayers every time I walk into the doctor's office. And I know that God loves me and wants me to serve Him in the land of the living. I really appreciate all the support you have given me and if you ever need me to pray for you when you're going through a trial or tribulation I'm here.

Because you see, it's not about me, it's about one person going through something and a whole bunch of people leaning on God and asking Him for healing that person. It's all about God's supernatural power and divine energy. Now I know that you all are thinking I'm way out there and I am. I have never in my life experienced this level of spirituality. I have never totally depended on God to carry me over a tight wire. I pray that that this may be a powerful testimony and that it may help you if you're experiencing a trial in life's unpredictable path.

Yours Truly,
Hope Alaniz

After I finished, I thought to myself, *did I really write this? Did all of these thoughts and words come from me? What a divine experience!* All I can tell you is that I didn't have to think about it. The words just flowed out.

Just about everyone who received the letter called and said they had been touched by what I had shared. Some wondered how I could be so open about something so personal.

All I know is that God wanted me to share the experience, to speak about the unspeakable, to shed light onto a dark illness, and to testify to his love, mercy, and hope.

the time had come

Once I had made the decision, I felt a wonderful sense of peace. I had received a lot of prayer from my friends, family, and church members. I had placed my life and future in God's hands and felt ready for whatever lay ahead. But Satan wasn't ready to admit defeat.

While I was being prepped for my surgery, Marc asked me if I was sure I wanted to go through with it. He told me that there was still time to back out and that I didn't have to have the surgery. I was sure he was just having last-minute jitters and second thoughts. So I told him not to confuse me. I assured him that we had made the right decision and that I would see him afterward.

I was told later that the surgery took fourteen hours, a good deal longer than we had expected. But the doctors had performed a new procedure, and I was the first woman in San Antonio to have it done.

I woke up to find my friend, Patsy, sitting beside my bed, holding my hand, and praying. And I felt the Lord's presence.

One of my doctors said my body was very swollen right after surgery and that she was surprised that I was praising God instead of moaning. But that was only part of the miracle. I only had two hours of extreme pain; the rest of my recovery time was just uncomfortable.

Two days after the surgery, I woke up to find Nita and my father sitting in my room. She had flown our dad down from Arlington and rolled him into the hospital in a wheelchair. She felt that Dad needed to see for himself that I was alright. A few hours later, once they were assured that I was doing well, they went home.

My bladder had been screened for cancer cells after it was removed, and my surgeon was excited to tell me that it was clean.

You can imagine his surprise when I told him that I knew that the cancer had disappeared. When he asked how I knew, I told him about the dreams and vision. And he left my room astounded.

So why did I go through major surgery if I believed I had been healed?

Because leaving the bladder could trigger a recurrence of the cancer, and because my doctor explained that he would not feel comfortable treating me if it was not removed.

But also because we had prayed and left the decision in God's hands, and we felt that he wanted me to have the procedure—perhaps just so the doctor could be astounded, I don't know.

6
relationships

NOT EVERYONE rallied around me while I was ill. Some of the people I expected to support me were not there.

But I understood that cancer scares people and reminds them of their own mortality, and I didn't let it bother me. I just did what God would do. I prayed for them and loved them without any conditions. On the other hand, I was indescribably blessed by the people who did show up and stuck it out.

My sons kept me motivated, spiritually and emotionally. They prayed over me and for me and went to prayer support meetings with me.

Marc and the boys shaved their heads when mine was shaved. They were my cheerleaders and prayer warriors.

Do you know how special it is when a child prays for a parent? It's usually the reverse.

Mike laid hands on me and prayed with me about many spiritual and physical issues, even though he was in excruciating back pain the whole time I was going through my illness. I thank God for Christian sons who lean so strongly on him.

Another son, Dave, lives in Washington State. He couldn't visit as often as he wanted to.

But I could feel his prayers and knew he was recruiting people I didn't even know to pray.

My parents were so special. Marc did not want me to tell them that I had been diagnosed with cancer. I told him that I had to, even though they were sick. I knew they would feel cheated if I didn't tell them. Besides, I knew their prayers would be needed and that they were special in God's eyes. The pleas of praying parents are strong and powerful.

My brother and sisters, niece and nephews, and in-laws totally supported me. I received many telephone calls from them. They prayed for me earnestly and without ceasing. They also had their churches praying for me.

I also told my grandchildren about my diagnosis. I wanted them to know that I was sick and how important their prayers and support were to me, and their parents were comfortable with that. They watched me lose my hair and saw how the treatments made me feel.

My granddaughter, Mandy, saw me wearing so many scarves that she decided she was going to wear a scarf when her folks took her to Sea World. She never noticed that I was wearing the scarves to cover my baldness. She just saw her "Maga" wearing colorful scarves and thought they were very fashionable.

Deeply hurt by the loss of his sisters and powerless to fix my disease, Marc was unable to help me as much as I needed him to.

But I love him and asked God to heal him and soften his heart. I also had to come to the place of accepting that my husband is not God, nor can he replace him. Like me, he is only human. So I released him to deal with things on his own terms.

And with God's help and many prayers, Marc came through for me. He went with me to all my doctor visits, all the chemotherapy treatments, and never missed a beat on any of my health care.

He prayed earnestly for my recovery. We have both learned not to take each other for granted and love God no matter how bad the situation looks. This experience increased my husband's faith and made him a stronger Christian.

My ordeal also strengthened and deepened my relationships with co-workers like Terry, Aurora, and Carla, who let me talk out feelings I tended to hold in at home, because I didn't want my family to think that I was in pain, depressed, or feeling hopeless.

Talking freely helped me sort my thoughts. And after they listened, they prayed with me. I know it was especially hard on Terry because her father was gong through the same illness.

In turn, they were deeply touched by some of the things I shared with them, and I believe that God used me to inspire them as well.

Not everyone knew what to say or do, and so they offered pity. They meant well, but that was the last thing I needed. I refused to feel sorry for myself or to allow anyone else to feel sorry for me. Pity only steals our happiness, hope, and trust in the Lord.

My friendship with Patsy was special. She was a rock for me. She prayed for me and provided unconditional love and support. She is truly my sister in Christ who God placed in my life at just the right time. I had been there for her when she lost her husband, and she was there for me when I got cancer.

As important as all these people were, my trust was in God, not in man. He was the only one who could save and heal me. He lifted me up when I was down, listened to my heart and soul, answered my prayers, and demonstrated his love for me throughout the illness and recovery period.

7
recovery

THREE MONTHS after surgery, I was well enough to return to work.

I knew that God had healed me, even before my first chemotherapy treatment. And I knew that he wanted me to write this testimony—to share my fears, hopes, and faith and inspire and encourage others who are facing cancer.

Am I afraid that the cancer might come back?

No!

Whenever the thought comes into my head, I shove it back out. I knew a lady who had just gone through cancer, and she told me she was saving her wigs and scarves so she would already have them if she was diagnosed with the disease again. I refuse to do that. When God does something, he does it right, and there's no reason to question it.

life changes

Yes, I've had to make some physical adjustments. But I don't dwell on them.

Every year I have to have a CT scan or MRI to see if there are any tumors in my abdominal area. As the machine scans, I pray:

> *"Our Father who art in heaven....(Breathe in)...hallowed be thy name...(Hold your breath).....thy kingdom come, thy will be done....(Breathe out)..."*

And this will be my routine for the rest of my life. But I'm okay with that.

I also have accepted the changes in my body, soul, and spirit. But life is all about change. And when we embrace it, we grow stronger.

Now, I live a day at a time, enjoying each moment, waking up to each new day, and trying to learn something new everyday.

God gave me a second chance, a new life, and I want it to please him. I want him to nudge the angels and point down to earth and say, "Look at Hope. She believed me, and I healed her. I made her whole again. I lifted her up when she was down. I tested her, like my servant, Job, and she passed the test. How I love her!"

Life's problems didn't end when I was well enough to return to work. I have had other health issues and family problems, just like anyone else.

I recently lost my father, and I want to be there for my mother. And there will be many other trials and challenges in my life.

But God carried me through one of the worst times, and I know he will carry me through whatever lies ahead, because that's how he is.

Sometimes, I even think that cancer might have been one of the best things that ever happened to me. And I laugh because I know that must really make the devil mad, because once again, what Satan intended for evil, God turned to good. The Lord has been glorified and praised in many lives because he showed himself faithful and victorious in mine.

Why did God heal me? I don't know. Why were my prayers answered? Only God knows. Maybe he just wanted one more testimony of faith.

I titled this booklet *The Seeds of Hope* because we are always planting seeds in our lives, like my family planted seeds in our vegetable garden.

Whether the crop is good or bad depends on the quality of the seeds we plant and how we nurture them.

The scriptures and promises of God that I declared aloud, again and again, were seeds.

The prayers of family and friends for my healing were seeds. The prayers of family and friends for my healing were seeds. I nurtured them and refused to allow pests and critters like doubt, fear, and hopelessness to ravage my garden and destroy my crop. And, like our garden at home, I enjoyed the luscious fruit of healing and stronger faith, deeper relationships, and seeing others strengthened and encouraged.

8
life after cancer

IT HAS BEEN nearly nine years since I wrote this little book. And they brought many more challenges.

But my bout with cancer is a memorial marker in my life like the stones and altars Israel set up to remind them of God's mighty miracles. So now, when life's storms rage,

I look back to my miraculous healing from cancer and remind myself of God's love, power, and faithfulness. And my faith leaps to its feet, ready to fight.

wonderful discovery

About three years ago, I found out that Marc had been suffering from Post Traumatic Stress Disorder (PTSD), resulting from his tour in Vietnam, the whole time we've been married.

After he retired and I was diagnosed with cancer, the PTSD escalated. But neither of us understood that at the time.

No wonder he had so much anger and anxiety during my ordeal. I realize now how strong and courageous he really was, staying by my side while he was being beaten down by his own invisible disease.

Today, through prayer, medication, counseling, and Bible study, he too has been completely healed! And our marriage is stronger than ever. God is so good!

the devil never quits; neither does God!

A year and a half ago, I was in the intensive care unit at our local hospital. After taking a couple of steroid shots in one knee, my sugars went through the roof. The doctors said I should have been in a coma. For many days, my glucose level would not come down.

Finally, Marc and I went down to the chapel and asked the Lord to normalize my blood sugar. We prayed fervently, went back up, and I laid down to take a nap.

Then the nurse came in and informed us that my sugars were way down and, if they stayed down, I could go home. And we were home that evening. Another memorial marker!

So, I'm still alive. Still writing. Still praising God and praying and mentoring and being a spiritual cheerleader for others who are passing through the valley of the shadow of death.

God is still using me to give hope. And Satan is still kicking himself for his failures.

My prayer is that, long after I leave this world, this little book continues to make the rounds—planting seeds of hope in the lives of people who are trying to find light.

There is life after cancer. And if you plant the right seeds, there is also joy and peace and laughter, purpose and fulfillment through Jesus Christ, our Lord. Amen.

Appendix A

Prayer for deliverance and bondage from cancer

"Are you hurting? Pray. Do you feel great? Sing. Are you sick? Call the church leaders together to pray and anoint you with oil in the name of the Master. Believing-prayer will heal you, and Jesus will put you on your feet."

~ James 5:14
The Message (paraphrase of the Holy Bible
Eugene H. Peterson

"We have to pray with our eyes on God, not on the difficulties."

~ Oswald Chambers

"Those persons who know the deep peace of God, the unfathomable peace that passeth all understanding, are always men and women of much prayer."

~ R.A. Torrey

"Don't pray when you feel like it. Have an appointment with the Lord and keep it. A man is powerful on his knees."

~ Corrie ten Boom

Dear Father in Heaven,

I/we boldly come before you and ask for healing for (NAME). Through Jesus Christ of Nazareth, and in the authority of his name, I/we boldly stand in agreement with (NAME) to bind and cast out the spirit of cancer.

In the name and by the authority of Jesus Christ, I/we command the cancer to disintegrate—seed, root, and cells.

I/we command this body to produce healthy blood, and I/we release healing and restoration to every normal cell and system and pray for protection of the mind and spirit. I/we command this body's defensive cells to attack, destroy, and dissolve every invading cancer cell.

Father, I/we also pray for (NAME's) family, friends, and loved ones. Give them patience and courage, wisdom, and guidance. Because illness gives Satan a foothold to steal, kill, and destroy, I/we bind and disallow these attacks. I/we pray light over this situation and place a hedge of protection around (NAME) and his/her family.

Throughout all these requests, Father, I/we pray that your will is done. I/we pray for all the doctors, nurses, oncologists, hospitals, and medical staff who are providing medical assistance and care. And I/we pray for divine wisdom, knowledge, and guidance in the decision-making process of (NAME's) medical care.

Holy Spirit, I/we ask you to be with (NAME) throughout his/her journey and provide comfort, rest, and peace in his/her soul, mind, and body, thereby displacing anger, fear, resentment, stress, anxiety, unforgiveness, and restlessness.

Father God, I/we request that you open doors for (NAME) financially and take care of all his/her medical expenses.

I/we also pray that you would send godly friends, family and church members, and support groups to stand with (NAME) against loneliness and depression. Show (NAME) that, even though he/she feels unattractive, he/she is handsome/beautiful in your eyes. And assure (NAME) in every way that you know his/her pain, feel compassion, and hear his/her prayers. I/we place a helmet over (NAME's) mind to protect against unhealthy and negative thoughts, self-talk, comments, or criticism from friends, family, or medical staff.

Finally, Father I/we pray that this experience with cancer helps (NAME) to become a bold warrior and a living testimony for your glory and honor. And I/we pray that (NAME) will have a renewing of his/her mind, soul, and spirit and be a "victor" instead of a "victim."

In the Name of Jesus Christ of Nazareth,

Amen.

Appendix B

I prayed these Scriptures and many more every day during my quiet times, desiring and believing for a miraculous healing from God. Faith comes by hearing and hearing by the word of God.[6] *And God's word did not return void. It accomplished what it was sent out to do.*

Genesis 20: 17—Then Abraham prayed to God, and God healed Abimelech, his wife and his slave girls so they could have children again.

Exodus 15: 26—I am the Lord, who heals you.

Job 5: 18—For he wounds, but he also binds up; he injures, but his hands also heal.

Psalm 30: 2—O Lord my God, I called to you for help and you healed me.

Isaiah 53:5—But he was pierced for our transgressions, he was crushed for our iniquities; the punishment that brought us peace was upon him, and by his wounds we are healed.

Malachi 4:2—But for you who revere my name, the sun of righteousness will rise with healing in its wings. And you will go out and leap like calves released from the stall.

---

[6] Romans 10:17.

Matthew 4:23—Jesus went throughout Galilee, teaching in their synagogues, preaching the good news of the kingdom, and healing every disease and sickness among the people.

Matthew 8:8,13—The centurion replied, "Lord, I do not deserve to have you come under my roof. But just say the word, and my servant will be healed. . . . Then Jesus said to the centurion, 'Go! It will be done just as you believed it would." And his servant was healed at that very hour.

Matthew 8:16-17-When evening came, many who were demon-possessed were brought to him, and he drove out the spirits with a word and healed all the sick. This was to fulfill what was spoken through the prophet Isaiah: "He took up our infirmities and carried our diseases."

Matthew 9:35—Jesus went through all the towns and villages, teaching in their synagogues, preaching the good news of the kingdom and healing every disease and sickness.

Matthew 12:22—Then they brought him a demon-possessed man who was blind and mute, and Jesus healed him, so that he could both talk and see.

Matthew 14:14—When Jesus landed and saw a large crowd, he had compassion on them and healed their sick.

Matthew 15:30—Great crowds came to him, bringing the lame, the blind, the crippled, the mute and many others, and laid them at his feet; and he healed them.

-Mark 5:29—Immediately her bleeding stopped and she felt in her body that she was freed from her suffering.

Luke 8:48—Then he said to her, "Daughter, your faith has healed you. Go in peace."

Acts 3:6-11—Then Peter said, "Silver or gold I do not have, but what I have I give you. In the name of Jesus Christ of Nazareth, walk." Taking him by the right hand, he helped him up, and instantly the man's feet and ankles became strong. He jumped to his feet and began to walk. Then he went with them into the temple courts, walking and jumping, and praising God When all the people saw him walking and praising God, they recognized him as the same man who used to sit begging at the temple gate called Beautiful, and they were filled with wonder and amazement at what had happened to him. While the beggar held on to Peter and John, all the people were astonished and came running to them in the place called Solomon's Colonnade.

Acts 5:16—Crowds gathered also from the towns around Jerusalem, bringing their sick and those tormented by evil spirits, and all of them were healed.

James 5:16 – Therefore confess your sins to each other and pray for each other so that you may be healed. The prayer of a righteous man is powerful and effective.

Made in the USA
San Bernardino, CA
24 February 2015